Better Homes and Gardens®

MEXICAN RECIPES

Our seal assures you that every recipe in *Mexican Recipes*
has been tested in the Better Homes and Gardens® Test Kitchen.
This means that each recipe is practical and reliable,
and meets our high standards of taste appeal.

For years, Better Homes and Gardens® has been a leader in publishing cook books. In *Mexican Recipes* we've pulled together a delicious collection of recipes from several of our latest best-sellers. These no-fail recipes will make your cooking easier and more enjoyable.

Editor: Rosemary C. Hutchinson
Editorial Project Manager: Marsha Jahns
Graphic Designer: Harijs Priekulis
Electronic Text Processor: Paula Forest

On the front cover: Cheese Quesadillas, Marinated Seafood, Cheese Crisps (see recipes, pages 42 and 44)

Contents

Spread dough so one of the long sides is at the long edge of the wrapper. Leave equal space at both ends (with the irregular shape of corn husks, the space at both ends may not be quite equal). Spoon filling down center.

Classic Tamales

12 corn husks *or* foil *or* parchment paper rectangles	● For wrappers, soak corn husks in warm water for several hours or overnight to soften. Pat with paper towels to remove excess moisture. (*Or,* cut foil or parchment into 8x6-inch rectangles.)
Tamale Dough (see recipe, page 6)	● Spoon a scant ¼ *cup* of dough onto *each* tamale wrapper. Spread dough into a 5x4-inch rectangle, spreading 1 long side of dough to edge of wrapper and leaving equal spaces at both ends.
Tamale Filling (see recipe, page 6)	● Spoon tamale filling lengthwise down center of dough, bringing filling out to both ends. Fold long edge of wrapper *over* filling so it overlaps dough about ½ inch, then continue rolling up wrapper jelly-roll style. Seal ends securely (see photo, right).
	● Place tamales on a steamer basket in an electric skillet. Add water to just below basket level, then bring to boiling. Cover and steam tamales at medium heat for 45 to 50 minutes or till tamales pull away from wrappers. (Add more water as necessary.) Unwrap tamales and serve immediately. Makes 12 tamales.

When you're using a foil wrapper, fold the ends underneath. For parchment paper or corn-husk wrappers, twist the ends and tie with string to seal.

Fold the long edge of the wrapper *over* the filling so it overlaps dough about ½ inch. Continue rolling up wrapper jelly-roll style. Tie ends with pieces of corn husk or string.

Steam tamales in an electric skillet (as shown) or use a Chinese steamer basket over a wok or saucepan. Remember to add boiling water to the skillet, wok, or saucepan as necessary, but avoid peeking, as this lets steam escape.

Savory Chicken Tamales

Pictured on pages 4–5.

12	corn husks *or* foil *or* parchment paper rectangles	● For wrappers, soak corn husks in warm water for several hours or overnight to soften. Pat with paper towels to remove excess moisture. (*Or,* cut foil or parchment into 8x6-inch rectangles.)

Tamales are "fiesta food" in Mexico. Filled with meat, they make a hearty meal, but stuff them with sweets, and they're an irresistible dessert or between-meal snack.

2¼	cups Masa Harina tortilla flour	● For tamale dough, in a large mixing bowl stir together tortilla flour and water. Cover and let stand for 20 minutes.
1	cup warm water	
¾	cup shortening *or* lard	In a large mixer bowl beat together shortening or lard and salt till fluffy. Beat in flour mixture till well combined.
¼	teaspoon salt	

● Spoon a scant *¼ cup* dough onto *each* tamale wrapper. Spread dough into a 5x4-inch rectangle, spreading 1 long side of the dough to the *edge* of the wrapper and leaving equal spaces at both ends (see photo, pages 4–5).

	Red Chili Sauce (see recipe, page 27) *or* Picante Sauce (see recipe, page 26)	● Spoon a scant *1 tablespoon* Red Chili Sauce or Picante Sauce lengthwise down the center of dough, bringing sauce out to both ends (see photo, pages 4–5). Top with about *1 tablespoon* chicken.
1	cup finely chopped cooked chicken	

● Fold long edge of wrapper *over* filling so it overlaps dough about ½ inch, then continue rolling up wrapper jelly-roll style. Tie ends securely with pieces of corn husk or string. *Or,* for foil, fold ends under to seal. (See photo, pages 4–5.)

● Place tamales on a steamer basket in an electric skillet. Add water to just below the basket level, then bring to boiling. Cover and steam tamales at medium heat for 35 to 40 minutes or till tamales pull away from the wrappers. (Add more water as necessary.)

Unwrap tamales. Serve immediately with remaining warm Red Chili Sauce or Picante Sauce. Makes 12 tamales.

Super Burritos

1 pound ground beef,
   Homemade Chorizo (see
   recipe, page 10), *or*
   bulk chorizo
1 cup chopped onion
½ cup chopped green pepper
1 clove garlic, minced
¼ cup water
1 tablespoon chili powder
¼ teaspoon ground cumin
1 cup cooked rice
1 4-ounce can diced green
   chili peppers, drained

● For filling, in a large skillet cook ground beef or chorizo, onion, green pepper, and garlic till meat is brown and onion is tender. Drain off fat.

Stir in water, chili powder, and cumin. Cook about 5 minutes or till most of the water has evaporated. Remove skillet from heat. Stir in rice and *half* of the chili peppers. (Use remaining peppers in Burrito Sauce, below).

Transform Super Burritos into Super Chimichangas by folding and frying the filled tortillas according to the directions in Beef Chimichangas (see recipe and photo, pages 12 and 13).

8 10-inch Flour Tortillas
   (see recipe, page 37) *or*
   purchased flour tortillas
1 cup shredded cheddar
   cheese (4 ounces)
1 medium tomato, chopped

● Stack tortillas and wrap tightly in foil. Heat in a 350° oven for 10 minutes to soften. (When ready to fill tortillas, remove only *half* at a time, keeping remainder warm in oven.)

Spoon a scant ½ *cup* filling onto *each* tortilla, just below center. Top *each* with cheese and tomato. Fold bottom edge of each tortilla up and over filling just till mixture is covered. Fold opposite sides of each tortilla in, just till they meet. Roll up tortillas from the bottom. Secure with wooden toothpicks.

Shredded lettuce
Burrito Sauce
Shredded cheddar cheese
Guacamole (see recipe,
   page 22) *or* frozen
   avocado dip, thawed

● Arrange burritos on a baking sheet. Bake in a 350° oven for 10 to 12 minutes or till heated through.

Remove toothpicks. Serve burritos on lettuce with Burrito Sauce, cheddar cheese, and Guacamole or avocado dip. Makes 4 servings.

● **Burrito Sauce:** In a medium saucepan melt 2 tablespoons *butter* or *margarine*. Stir in 1 tablespoon *all-purpose flour*. Add 1 cup *chicken broth* all at once. Cook and stir over medium heat till thickened and bubbly, then cook and stir for 1 minute more. Stir 2 tablespoons *all-purpose flour* into one 8-ounce carton dairy *sour cream*. Stir sour cream and remaining *green chili peppers* into sauce. Cook and stir till thickened and bubbly, then cook and stir for 1 minute more.

Chicken Flautas

Ingredients	Instructions
2 whole medium chicken breasts (about 1½ pounds total) **1 cup water** **1 cup shredded Monterey Jack *or* cheddar cheese (4 ounces)** **1 4-ounce can diced green chili peppers, drained** **½ teaspoon ground cumin**	● Place chicken breasts in a large saucepan. Add water and bring to boiling. Reduce heat and simmer, covered, for 20 to 25 minutes or till chicken is tender. Drain well. Let stand till chicken is cool enough to handle. Skin and bone chicken breasts. Use a fork to pull chicken apart into long thin shreds (you should have about 2¼ cups). In a medium mixing bowl stir together shredded chicken, cheese, chili peppers, and cumin. Set mixture aside.
16 8-inch Flour Tortillas (see recipe, page 37) *or* purchased flour tortillas	● Stack tortillas and wrap tightly in foil. Heat in a 350° oven for 10 minutes to soften. (When ready to fill tortillas, remove only *half* at a time, keeping remainder warm in oven.)
	● For each flauta, overlap *2* softened tortillas by about half. Spoon about *⅓ cup* of the chicken mixture lengthwise down center of overlapped tortillas. Roll up tortillas lengthwise as tightly as possible (see photo, right). Secure with wooden toothpicks.
Cooking oil	● In a heavy 10- or 12-inch skillet (or an electric skillet) heat about ½ inch of oil to 365°. Fry rolled-up tortillas, 2 or 3 at a time, for 3 to 4 minutes total or till crisp and golden brown. Drain on paper towels. Keep flautas warm in a 300° oven while frying remaining tortillas.
Shredded lettuce **Guacamole (see recipe, page 22) *or* frozen avocado dip, thawed** **Dairy sour cream** **Homemade Salsa (see recipe, page 24) *or* purchased salsa** **Hot pepper slices (optional)**	● Remove toothpicks. Serve flautas on shredded lettuce with Guacamole or avocado dip, sour cream, and Homemade Salsa or salsa. Garnish with hot pepper slices, if desired. Serves 4.

You'll play a new supper-time tune with these tightly rolled and fried tortillas that resemble "little flutes" from which they take their name.

Overlap a couple of tortillas by about half (the two overlapped tortillas need to measure about 8 inches long). Spoon filling lengthwise down the center and roll up tortillas very tightly.

It would take a mathematical wizard to compute all the different topping combinations for tacos, flautas, tostadas, enchiladas, burritos, or chimichangas. Here are our suggestions: chopped or sliced ripe olives, sliced radishes, chopped chili peppers (fresh, canned, or pickled), chopped tomatoes, or sliced green onion, and chunks or slices of avocado. Or, add your own favorite toppings.

Temper the flame from a hot and spicy combo with a topping of sour cream or mild guacamole, or both. (See our recipe, page 22, or use frozen avocado dip.) And if you want to *add* fuel to the fire, try one of our salsas, or a bottled taco sauce or salsa that's labeled *HOT*.

Finally, don't forget lots of shredded cheese to top off your Mexican meal!

Chorizo Tacos

8 6-inch corn tortillas
    or taco shells
    Cooking oil

● If using tortillas, in a heavy skillet heat ½ inch of oil. Fry each tortilla in hot oil for 10 seconds or till limp. Use tongs to fold tortilla in half. Continue frying for 1¼ to 1½ minutes or till crisp, turning once. Drain well on paper towels. Keep shells warm in a 300° oven while preparing meat mixture. (If using taco shells, warm in a 300° oven for 8 to 10 minutes before filling.)

Start with an already seasoned meat mixture for fast and easy tacos. Marinate the chicken in a lemon-honey mixture for a sensational taco meal.

1 pound Homemade
    Chorizo (see recipe,
    below), bulk chorizo,
    or bulk Italian sausage
    Shredded lettuce
    Guacamole (see recipe,
    page 22) *or* frozen
    avocado dip, thawed
¾ cup shredded Monterey
    Jack cheese (3 ounces)
1 large tomato, chopped

● In a medium skillet cook meat till brown. Drain off fat.
    Fill each taco shell with some of the meat, lettuce, Guacamole or avocado dip, cheese, and tomato. Serves 4.

Homemade Chorizo

1 3-pound boneless pork
    shoulder roast, well
    chilled

● Trim fat from chilled roast. Chop enough fat to make 1 cup and set aside. Discard any remaining fat.
    Cut meat into ½-inch cubes. Using a food processor or the coarse plate of a meat grinder, grind together pork and reserved pork fat.

Freeze hot-and-peppery Mexican sausage, chorizo (chor-EE-so), in ½-pound or 1-pound packages so it's easy to grab *just* what you need.

½   cup white vinegar
3   cloves garlic
2   tablespoons paprika
1   tablespoon chili powder
2½ teaspoons crushed red
     pepper
2   teaspoons ground red
     pepper
1   teaspoon sugar
½   teaspoon coriander seed
½   teaspoon dried oregano
¼   teaspoon ground cumin

● In a blender container or food processor bowl combine vinegar, garlic, paprika, chili powder, crushed red pepper, ground red pepper, sugar, coriander seed, oregano, cumin, 3 tablespoons *water,* 2 teaspoons *salt,* and 1 teaspoon *black pepper.* Cover and blend or process till spices are ground. Pour spice mixture over ground pork mixture. Mix till thoroughly combined.
    Cover and refrigerate meat for up to 4 days or freeze for up to 2 months. Makes about 3 pounds.

Marinated Chicken Tacos

¼ **cup lemon juice**
2 **tablespoons honey**
2 **tablespoons water**
1 **clove garlic, minced**
¼ **teaspoon pepper**
2 **cups chopped cooked chicken**

● For marinade, in a small bowl stir together lemon juice, honey, water, garlic, and pepper. Pour over chicken, stirring to coat well.
  Cover and marinate at room temperature for 30 minutes or in the refrigerator for 2 hours, stirring occasionally. Drain well.

Leftover chicken? Here's a great way to use it up. Marinate the chicken in a lemon-honey mixture for a sensational taco meal.

1 **cup alfalfa sprouts**
¼ **cup shredded carrot**

● In a small mixing bowl stir together alfalfa sprouts and carrot. Set aside.

8 **6-inch corn tortillas**
  or **taco shells**
  Cooking oil

● If using tortillas, in a heavy skillet heat ½ inch of oil. Fry each tortilla in hot oil for 10 seconds or till limp. Use tongs to fold tortilla in half. Continue frying for 1¼ to 1½ minutes or till crisp, turning once. Drain on paper towels. (If using taco shells, warm in a 300° oven for 8 to 10 minutes before filling.)

½ **cup crumbled blue cheese**
1 **large tomato, chopped**

● Fill each taco shell with some of the chicken, alfalfa-sprout-carrot mixture, cheese, and tomato. Makes 4 servings.

Let's Have A Taco Fiesta!

Come party time, no food fits the bill better than *tacos,* especially if you plan a do-it-yourself taco bar.

Arrange the taco fillings, toppers, and garnishes in pottery or wooden bowls. Buy packaged taco shells and serve them in baskets or gourds lined with brightly colored napkins.

Take your pick from an endless assortment of taco ingredients.
Fillings: ground beef or pork, shredded roast beef or pork, sausage, chicken, ham, or chili.

Toppers: chopped olives, green peppers, radishes, tomatoes, avocados, hot peppers, or onions.
Garnishes: sour cream, guacamole, taco sauce or salsa, shredded lettuce, and shredded cheese.

Refried beans are a must; serve them as fillings or as an extra side dish. Round out the menu with purchased Spanish rice and thirst-quenching Mexican beer. Finally, for an easy but satisfying finale, dish up ice cream and top it with coffee liqueur.

Use two forks to pull the
cooked meat into shreds.

Place filling near one
edge of tortilla and fold
that edge up and over the
filling.

Beef Chimichangas

1 **pound beef stew meat, cut into 1½-inch cubes** 1½ **cups water** 2 **cloves garlic, minced** ½ **teaspoon salt**	● In a medium saucepan combine meat, water, garlic, and salt. Bring to boiling; reduce heat. Cover and simmer about 1¼ hours or till meat is very tender. Uncover and boil rapidly for 10 to 12 minutes or till water has evaporated. Stir near end of cooking time to prevent meat from sticking. Remove from heat.	**Feature these beef-filled bundles at your next informal dinner party. Make them part of the fun by preparing the filling ahead and saving the assembling and frying until party time.**
1 **4-ounce can diced green chili peppers, drained** 1 **tablespoon vinegar** 2 **teaspoons chili powder** ¼ **teaspoon ground cumin** **Dash black pepper**	● Shred the cooked meat with 2 forks, or let cool and pull apart with your fingers. Combine with chili peppers, vinegar, chili powder, cumin, and black pepper. (If making filling ahead, cover and chill for up to 3 days. Heat till warm before filling tortillas.)	**If you want to have them finished for your guests, fry the chimichangas and refrigerate or freeze them. To reheat, just wrap each bundle in foil and bake in a 350° oven until heated through: 15 to 20 minutes if refrigerated and 30 to 35 minutes if frozen.**
6 **8- *or* 10-inch Flour Tortillas (see recipe, page 37) *or* purchased flour tortillas**	● Meanwhile, stack tortillas and wrap in foil; heat in a 350° oven for 10 minutes. Spoon about *⅓ cup* meat mixture onto each tortilla near 1 edge. Fold edge nearest filling up and over filling till mixture is almost covered. Fold in the 2 sides envelope-fashion, then roll up. Secure with wooden toothpicks.	
Cooking oil	● In a heavy skillet or saucepan fry 2 or 3 filled tortillas in 1 inch of hot cooking oil (375°) about 1 minute on each side or till golden brown. Drain on a rack or on paper towels. Keep warm in a 300° oven while frying remaining tortillas.	
2 **cups shredded lettuce** **Dairy sour cream** **Picante Sauce (see recipe, page 26) *or* purchased picante sauce**	● To serve, remove toothpicks. Place each chimichanga atop lettuce on a plate; top with sour cream and Picante Sauce. Garnish with pickled cherry peppers, if desired. Makes 6 servings.	

Roll up and secure with wooden toothpicks.

Fold in the two sides.

Quesadillas with Picadillo Filling

2 **tablespoons cooking oil** 1 **pound beef round steak, finely chopped** ½ **cup chopped onion** 1 **clove garlic, minced**	● In a large skillet heat 2 tablespoons oil; cook beef, onion, and garlic till beef is brown and onion is tender.
2 **medium tomatoes, peeled and chopped** 1 **medium apple, peeled, cored, and chopped** ½ **cup raisins** 1 **to 3 canned jalapeño peppers, drained and chopped** 2 **tablespoons vinegar** 1 **teaspoon sugar** 1 **teaspoon salt** ½ **teaspoon ground cinnamon** ⅛ **teaspoon ground cloves** ⅛ **teaspoon ground cumin**	● Stir in tomatoes, apple, raisins, jalapeño peppers, vinegar, sugar, salt, cinnamon, cloves, and cumin; simmer, covered, for 20 minutes.
½ **cup toasted slivered almonds**	● Stir in almonds; cook, uncovered, for 2 minutes more. Remove from heat.
12 **6-inch flour *or* corn tortillas** 2 **tablespoons cooking oil**	● Place about ¼ *cup* filling on each tortilla. Fold tortillas in half; secure each with a wooden toothpick, if desired. In a skillet heat 2 tablespoons cooking oil; cook filled tortillas, a few at a time, in the hot oil about 2 minutes per side or till light brown. Keep warm in a 300° oven while frying remaining tortillas.
2 **cups shredded lettuce** **Dairy sour cream** **Sliced green onions** **Radish roses**	● To serve, place 2 quesadillas atop some of the shredded lettuce on a plate. Garnish with sour cream, green onions, and radish roses. Makes 6 servings.

Don't let the big words in the title put you off. Quesadillas (kay-sah-DEE-yahs) are made with flour or corn tortillas and are something between a turnover and a grilled sandwich.

Picadillo (pee-kah-DEE-yoh) is a beef mixture made with tomato, onion, apple, raisins, nuts, and sweet spices. If you're not up to the heat of three jalapeños, use fewer jalapeños and remove the fiery ribs to which the pepper seeds are attached.

Chicken Tostadas

2 whole medium chicken breasts (about 1½ pounds total) 1 cup water	● Place chicken breasts in a large skillet. Add water and bring to boiling. Reduce heat and simmer, covered, for 20 to 25 minutes or till chicken is tender. Drain well. Let stand till cool enough to handle. Skin and bone chicken breasts. Use a fork to pull chicken apart into long, thin shreds (you should have about 2¼ cups). Set chicken aside.
2 cups shredded lettuce ⅓ cup shredded carrot 2 tablespoons salad oil 1 tablespoon lemon juice 1 tablespoon vinegar	● Meanwhile, in a medium mixing bowl combine lettuce and carrot. Stir together salad oil, lemon juice, and vinegar, then toss with lettuce mixture. Set aside.
Salsa *or* taco sauce 1 10½-ounce can jalapeño bean dip 1 large avocado, seeded, peeled, and cut up 1 tablespoon lemon juice	● In a small mixing bowl add enough salsa or taco sauce (about ½ cup) to bean dip to make it spreadable. In a small mixing bowl use a fork to mash avocado. Stir in lemon juice.
Cooking oil 6 6-inch corn tortillas	● In a heavy skillet heat about ¼ inch of oil. Fry tortillas, one at a time, in hot oil about 30 seconds on each side or till crisp and golden brown. Drain on paper towels. Keep tortillas warm in a 300° oven while frying the remainder.
¾ cup shredded cheddar *or* Monterey Jack cheese (3 ounces) 1 medium tomato, chopped ⅓ cup sliced pitted ripe olives	● Place tortillas on 6 dinner plates. Dividing ingredients equally among tortillas, layer ingredients in the following order: bean dip mixture, avocado, chicken, lettuce mixture, cheese, tomato, and olives. Makes 6 servings.

Enjoy the ultimate open-face sandwich. Just mound a crisp corn tortilla high with vegetables, chicken, and cheese.

Creamy Seafood Enchiladas

1 8-ounce package cream cheese, softened
½ cup shredded Monterey Jack cheese (2 ounces)
2 tablespoons dry white wine
2 6-ounce packages frozen crabmeat and shrimp, thawed and drained

● For filling, in a small mixer bowl combine cream cheese, Monterey Jack cheese, and wine. Beat with an electric mixer till almost smooth. Stir in crabmeat and shrimp.

2 tablespoons cooking oil
12 6-inch corn tortillas

● In a heavy skillet heat cooking oil. Dip tortillas, one at a time, in hot oil for 10 seconds or just till limp, adding more oil if needed. Drain on paper towels.

● Spoon about ¼ *cup* filling onto each tortilla, then roll up. Place the filled tortillas, seam side down, in a 13x9x2-inch baking dish.

½ cup sliced green onion
3 tablespoons butter *or* margarine
¼ cup all-purpose flour
¼ teaspoon salt
¼ teaspoon pepper
2¾ cups milk

● For sauce, in a medium saucepan cook onion in butter or margarine till tender but not brown. Stir in flour, salt, and pepper. Add milk all at once. Cook and stir till thickened and bubbly. Pour sauce over tortillas.

1 cup shredded Monterey Jack cheese (4 ounces)
Sliced green onion
Paprika

● Bake, covered, in a 350° oven for 15 to 20 minutes or till heated through. Remove foil and top with cheese. Return to oven and bake about 5 minutes more or till cheese melts. Garnish with green onion and paprika. Makes 6 servings.

Milk to put out a hot pepper fire? The oils that give hot peppers their zip dissolve in fat. So a swig of whole milk works better than skim milk, pop, or even water at dousing a hot pepper fire in your mouth. Another surefire remedy is beer—hot pepper oils also dissolve in alcohol.

Chicken Enchiladas

¼ **cup chopped pecans**
¼ **cup chopped onion**
2 **tablespoons butter** *or* **margarine**

● In a skillet cook ¼ cup pecans and onion in butter or margarine till onion is tender and pecans are lightly toasted. Remove from heat.

1 **3-ounce package cream cheese, softened**
1 **tablespoon milk**
½ **teaspoon salt**
¼ **teaspoon ground cumin**
2 **cups chopped cooked chicken**

● In a bowl combine softened cream cheese, 1 tablespoon milk, salt, and ground cumin. Add nut mixture and chopped cooked chicken. Stir together till well combined.

6 **8-inch Flour Tortillas (see recipe, page 37)** *or* **purchased flour tortillas**

● Spoon about ⅓ *cup* chicken mixture onto *each* tortilla near 1 edge; roll up. Place filled tortillas, seam side down, in a greased 12x7½x2-inch baking dish.

1 **10¾-ounce can condensed cream of chicken soup**
1 **8-ounce carton dairy sour cream**
1 **cup milk**
5 *or* 6 **pickled jalapeño peppers, rinsed, seeded, and chopped (⅓ cup)**

● In a bowl combine cream of chicken soup, sour cream, 1 cup milk, and the chopped pickled jalapeño peppers. Pour the soup mixture evenly over the tortillas in the baking dish. Cover with foil; bake in a 350° oven about 35 minutes or till heated through.

1 **cup shredded Monterey Jack** *or* **cheddar cheese (4 ounces)**
2 **tablespoons chopped pecans**

● Remove foil. Sprinkle enchiladas with cheese and 2 tablespoons pecans. Return to the 350° oven for 4 to 5 minutes or till cheese is melted. Makes 6 servings.

These nut-topped enchiladas are so rich and creamy that one of them makes an ample helping. Serve with a refreshing green or fruit salad and your favorite rice dish. Though the enchiladas are fairly mild, you may want to have a cold beverage handy to put out an occasional jalapeño fire.

Texas Chili

2½ pounds beef round steak, cut into ½-inch cubes
2 tablespoons cooking oil
1 medium onion, chopped
¼ cup crushed red pepper
2 cloves garlic, minced
1½ teaspoons ground cumin

● In a large saucepan brown *half* of the meat in hot oil. With a slotted spoon, remove meat; set aside. Add remaining meat, onion, red pepper, garlic, and cumin; cook till meat is brown. Return all meat to saucepan.

1 10½-ounce can condensed beef broth
1 soup can (1⅓ cups) water
½ teaspoon dried oregano, crushed
Hot cooked Pinto Beans

● Stir in beef broth, water, and oregano. Bring to boiling; reduce heat. Simmer, uncovered, for 1 to 1¼ hours or till meat is tender, stirring occasionally. Serve the chili with hot cooked Pinto Beans. Makes 6 to 8 servings.

● **Pinto Beans:** Rinse 1 pound (2½ cups) dry *pinto beans*. In a large saucepan or Dutch oven combine beans and 6 cups *water*. Cover and soak overnight. (Or, bring to boiling; reduce heat. Simmer for 2 minutes. Remove from heat. Cover; let stand for 1 hour.) Drain. In the same pan combine drained beans; 6 cups more *water;* 2 cloves *garlic,* minced; 1½ teaspoons *salt;* and ¼ teaspoon *black pepper.* Bring to boiling; reduce heat. Cover and simmer for 1½ to 2 hours or till tender; drain. Makes 6 cups.

Texans are touchy about their chili. They use cubed beef instead of ground beef, and if they use beans, they serve them with, not in, the chili. The chili's red color comes from pure ground chili peppers, not tomato. Texans seem to have a high tolerance for hot and spicy foods, so if you're not from the Lone Star State, taste at your own risk.

TNT Chili

2 pounds lean ground beef 2 medium onions, chopped 1 medium green pepper, 　seeded and chopped 1 stalk celery, chopped 1 clove garlic, minced	● In a large saucepan or Dutch oven cook ground beef, onions, green pepper, celery, and garlic till meat is brown and vegetables are tender; do not drain.
2 16-ounce cans tomatoes, 　cut up 1 15-ounce can tomato 　sauce 1½ cups water 6 *or* 7 pickled jalapeño 　peppers, rinsed and 　chopped (½ cup) ¼ cup chili powder 1 tablespoon ground red 　pepper ½ teaspoon salt ½ teaspoon black pepper 1 bay leaf	● Stir in *undrained* tomatoes, tomato sauce, water, rinsed and chopped jalapeño peppers, chili powder, ground red pepper, salt, black pepper, and bay leaf. Bring mixture to boiling; reduce heat. Simmer, uncovered, for 1½ hours, stirring occasionally.
1 15½-ounce can red kidney 　beans, drained	● Stir in beans; cook for 30 minutes more. Remove bay leaf before serving. Makes 8 to 10 servings.

Dynamite Chili: Prepare TNT Chili as directed above, *except* use 4 or 5 *pickled jalapeño peppers* (⅓ cup chopped) and 2 teaspoons *ground red pepper.*
Firecracker Chili: Prepare TNT Chili as directed above, *except* use 2 or 3 *pickled jalapeño peppers* (¼ cup chopped) and 1½ teaspoons *ground red pepper.*

Here's a chili you can gear up or down to suit your tolerance for explosives. *TNT, Dynamite,* and *Firecracker Chili* each contain ¼ *cup* chili powder, but vary in the number of jalapeños and amounts of ground red pepper.
　TNT Chili was judged "extra hot" by our panel of hot-food enthusiasts. One of the tasters began to sweat after a few bites. All of the panelists agreed that each bite was noticeably hotter than the last, but enjoyed the chili down to the last spoonful.

FAJITAS

Assembling your own fajita (fah-HEE-tuh) is like filling a taco. Pile a warm flour tortilla with bite-size strips of chicken or marinated skirt steak, then top with guacamole, salsa, cheese, and any other condiments you like. Roll it up and you've got yourself a fajita. (By the way, fajita aficionados claim that the chicken or beef *must* be brought to the table sizzling hot or it's not a true South Texas fajita.)

Spicy-Hot Chicken Fajitas
(see recipe, page 23)

Sizzling Beef Fajitas

1 to 1¼ pounds boneless beef plate skirt steak, flank steak, *or* round steak
½ cup Italian salad dressing
½ cup Homemade Salsa (see recipe, page 24) *or* purchased salsa
2 tablespoons soy sauce

● Partially freeze beef. Thinly slice across the grain into thin bite-size strips and set aside.

For marinade, in a large mixing bowl stir together salad dressing, salsa, and soy sauce. Add beef, stirring to coat. Cover and marinate in the refrigerator for 6 hours or overnight, stirring occasionally. Drain beef well.

8 8-inch Flour Tortillas (see recipe, page 37) *or* purchased flour tortillas

● Stack tortillas and wrap in foil. Heat in a 350° oven for 10 minutes to soften.

1 tablespoon cooking oil
1 small onion, thinly sliced and separated into rings
1 medium green pepper, cut into thin strips

● Meanwhile, preheat a 10-inch skillet over medium-high heat, then add oil (add more oil as necessary during cooking). Cook and stir onion rings in hot oil for 1½ minutes. Add green pepper strips. Cook and stir for 1½ minutes or till vegetables are crisp-tender. Remove vegetables from skillet.

● Add *half* of the beef to the hot skillet. Cook and stir for 2 to 3 minutes or till done. Remove beef. Cook and stir remaining beef for 2 to 3 minutes. Drain well. Return all beef and vegetables to skillet. Cook and stir for 1 to 2 minutes or till heated through.

Guacamole (see recipe, right) *or* frozen avocado dip, thawed
Homemade Salsa *or* Pico de Gallo Salsa (see recipes, pages 24 and 27), *or* purchased salsa
Dairy sour cream
Shredded cheddar cheese

● To serve, immediately fill warmed tortillas with beef-vegetable mixture, then add Guacamole or avocado dip, salsa, sour cream, and cheese. Roll fajitas up. Makes 4 servings.

Guacamole: In a blender container or food processor bowl combine 2 medium *avocados,* seeded, peeled, and cut up; 1 medium *tomato,* peeled, seeded, and coarsely chopped; ½ small *onion,* cut up; 1 tablespoon chopped *serrano or jalapeño pepper;* 1 tablespoon snipped *cilantro or parsley;* 1 tablespoon *lemon or lime juice;* and ¼ teaspoon *salt.*

Cover and blend or process till well combined, stopping machine occasionally to scrape down sides. Transfer mixture to a serving bowl. Cover and chill. Use as a dip for chips or as a topper for main dishes. Makes about 1¾ cups.

Spicy-Hot Chicken Fajitas

Pictured on pages 20–21.

Once you've tried the traditional *beef* fajitas, branch out and sink your teeth into a couple of these surprisingly spicy *chicken* fajitas.

3 whole medium chicken breasts (about 2¼ pounds total), skinned and boned ½ cup hot-style tomato juice *or* tomato juice 1 to 2 tablespoons chopped canned jalapeño peppers 2 teaspoons cornstarch ½ teaspoon instant chicken bouillon granules	● Cut chicken into thin bite-size strips and set aside. For sauce, in a small mixing bowl stir together tomato juice, jalapeño peppers, cornstarch, and bouillon granules. Set sauce mixture aside.
8 8-inch Flour Tortillas (see recipe, page 37) *or* purchased flour tortillas	● Stack tortillas and wrap in foil. Heat in a 350° oven for 10 minutes to soften.
1 tablespoon cooking oil 1 small zucchini, cut into 2-inch-long julienne strips (about 1½ cups) 3 green onions, bias-sliced into 1-inch lengths (about ½ cup)	● Meanwhile, preheat a 10-inch skillet over medium-high heat, then add oil (add more oil as necessary during cooking). Cook and stir zucchini in hot oil for 30 seconds. Add onion and cook and stir for 1½ minutes or till vegetables are crisp-tender. Remove from skillet.
	● Add *half* of the chicken to the hot skillet. Cook and stir for 2 to 3 minutes or till done. Remove chicken. Cook and stir remaining chicken for 2 to 3 minutes. Return all chicken to skillet. Push the chicken from the center of the skillet.
1 medium tomato, cut into thin wedges	● Stir sauce, then add to the center of skillet. Cook and stir till thickened and bubbly, then cook and stir for 1 minute more. Return vegetables to skillet. Stir ingredients together to coat with sauce. Arrange tomato atop. Cover and cook for 1 minute.
Guacamole (see recipe, opposite) *or* frozen avocado dip, thawed Pico de Gallo Salsa (see recipe, page 27) Dairy sour cream Shredded cheddar cheese	● To serve, immediately fill warmed tortillas with chicken-vegetable mixture, then add Guacamole or avocado dip, Pico de Gallo Salsa, sour cream, and cheese. Roll fajitas up. Makes 4 servings.

Salsa Verde

5 *or* 6 fresh tomatillos,
   finely chopped, *or* one
   13-ounce can tomatillos,
   drained, rinsed, and
   finely chopped
2 tablespoons finely
   chopped onion
1 serrano *or* jalapeño
   pepper, seeded and
   finely chopped
1 teaspoon snipped cilantro
   or parsley
¼ teaspoon salt

● In a small mixing bowl stir together tomatillos, onion, serrano or jalapeño pepper, cilantro or parsley, and salt. Cover and chill for several hours or overnight, stirring occasionally.

Store, tightly covered, in the refrigerator for up to 2 days. Use as a dip for chips or as a topping for main dishes. Makes about ¾ cup sauce.

Tomatillos and fresh cilantro lend their distinctive flavors to this green sauce. Try it over chicken or pork tacos.

Homemade Salsa

3 medium tomatoes, peeled
   and finely chopped
   (about 2 cups)
1 4-ounce can diced green
   chili peppers, drained
¼ cup sliced green onion
¼ cup chopped green
   pepper
2 tablespoons lemon juice
1 to 2 tablespoons snipped
   cilantro *or* parsley
1 clove garlic, minced
⅛ teaspoon pepper
½ cup tomato sauce

● In a medium mixing bowl stir together tomatoes, chili peppers, green onion, green pepper, lemon juice, cilantro or parsley, garlic, and pepper.

Place about *1 cup* of the tomato mixture and tomato sauce in a blender container or food processor bowl. Cover and blend or process just till pureed. Stir into remaining tomato mixture. Cover and chill for several hours or overnight, stirring occasionally.

Store, tightly covered, in the refrigerator for up to 3 days. Use as a dip for chips or as a topping for main dishes. Makes about 3⅓ cups sauce.

Salsas are the salt and pepper of Mexico and the American Southwest. No table is set without several bowls of salsa, ranging from mild to searing. (You'll find ours falls in the middle range.) Use it on everything from soups to nachos.

Red Chili Sauce
(see recipe, page 27)

Salsa Verde

Homemade Salsa

Ranchero Salsa

2 slices bacon	● In a medium skillet cook bacon till crisp. Drain, reserving drippings. Crumble bacon and set aside.
½ cup chopped onion 1 clove garlic, minced 3 medium tomatoes, seeded and chopped (about 2 cups) 1 canned jalapeño pepper, drained, seeded, and chopped ¼ teaspoon sugar ¼ teaspoon ground cumin	● Cook onion and garlic in reserved drippings till tender but not brown. Stir in tomatoes, jalapeño pepper, sugar, and cumin. Cover and cook over medium heat for 3 minutes. Uncover and simmer for 10 minutes or till most of the liquid has evaporated. Stir in bacon. Store, tightly covered, in the refrigerator for up to 3 days. Use as topping for main dishes. Makes about 1⅓ cups.

Pep up your morning by spooning Ranchero Salsa over scrambled eggs, poached eggs, or a cheese soufflé.

Picante Sauce

4 medium tomatoes, seeded and cut up 1 medium onion, cut up 2 cloves garlic 1 to 2 jalapeño *or* serrano peppers 2 tablespoons snipped cilantro *or* parsley 1 teaspoon celery seed	● Place tomatoes in a blender container or food processor bowl. Cover and blend or process till coarsely ground. Add onion, garlic, jalapeño or serrano peppers, cilantro or parsley, and celery seed. Cover and blend or process till finely ground.
1 medium green pepper, finely chopped 2 tablespoons vinegar 1 teaspoon salt 1 teaspoon sugar ½ teaspoon dried oregano, crushed ⅛ teaspoon ground cumin	● Transfer tomato mixture to a medium saucepan. Stir in green pepper, vinegar, salt, sugar, oregano, and cumin. Bring tomato mixture to boiling. Reduce heat and simmer, uncovered, for 30 to 40 minutes or to desired consistency.
	● Store, tightly covered, in the refrigerator for up to 2 weeks. Use as a dip for chips or a topping for main dishes. Makes about 2⅔ cups sauce.

Use this fiery topping like barbecue sauce and brush it onto ribs or burgers during the last 10 to 15 minutes of grilling.

Red Chili Sauce *Pictured on page 25.*

6 dried ancho peppers *or*
  ¼ cup chili powder
2 tablespoons cooking
    oil
	● If using dried peppers, cut open and discard stems and seeds. Cut peppers into small pieces. Place in a bowl and cover with boiling water. Let stand for 45 to 60 minutes or till pliable. Drain well. *Or,* if using chili powder, cook and stir chili powder in hot oil over medium-low heat for 4 minutes. (Omit the cooking oil if using dried peppers.)

1 14½-ounce can tomatoes
2 cloves garlic
2 teaspoons sugar
½ teaspoon salt
½ teaspoon dried oregano,
    crushed
¼ teaspoon ground cumin
	● Place *undrained* tomatoes in a blender container or food processor bowl. Add drained peppers or chili powder mixture and garlic. Cover and blend or process till smooth. Transfer to a saucepan. Stir in sugar, salt, oregano, and cumin. Bring to boiling. Reduce heat and simmer, uncovered, for 10 minutes or till slightly thickened.
	   Store, tightly covered, in the refrigerator for up to 2 weeks. Serve warm as topping for main dishes. Makes 1½ cups.

Molcajete and Tejolote. Sound like a comedy team? It's really the three-legged Mexican version of a mortar and pestle (pictured on page 25). Mexican cooks still prepare thick and chunky guacamoles and salsas with these volcanic rock tools just as they did 3,500 years ago.

Green Chili Sauce

¼ cup chopped onion
1 clove garlic, minced
1 tablespoon cooking oil
3 medium tomatoes, peeled
    and chopped
1 4-ounce can diced green
    chili peppers, drained
1 tablespoon snipped
    cilantro *or* parsley
	● In a medium skillet cook onion and garlic in hot oil till onion is tender but not brown. Stir in tomatoes, chili peppers, cilantro or parsley, ¼ teaspoon *salt,* and dash *pepper.* Simmer for 10 to 15 minutes or till slightly thickened.
	   Store, tightly covered, in the refrigerator for up to 3 days. Serve warm as topping for main dishes. Makes about 1½ cups.

Take a tip from our Test Kitchen: Before peeling a tomato, spear it with a fork and plunge it into boiling water for 20 to 30 seconds. Immediately dip it in cold water; the peel slips right off.

Pico de Gallo Salsa

2 medium tomatoes, peeled
    and finely chopped
2 tablespoons finely
    chopped onion
2 tablespoons snipped
    cilantro *or* parsley
1 serrano pepper, finely
    chopped
    Dash sugar
	● In a medium mixing bowl stir together chopped tomatoes, onion, cilantro or parsley, serrano pepper, and sugar. Cover and chill for several hours or overnight, stirring occasionally.
	   Store, tightly covered, in the refrigerator for up to 3 days. Use as a dip for chips or a topping for main dishes. Makes 1¼ cups.

Nobody knows how this salsa inherited its name, because Pico de Gallo (PEE-koh day GAH-yoh) is also the name for a traditional Latin American jicama and orange salad.
   The name, which means "rooster's beak," refers to the old-style way of eating the salad by picking up chunks with your fingers—the way a rooster pecks corn.

Chicken with Mole Sauce

2	dried ancho, mulato, *or* pasilla peppers, *or* a combination of 2 varieties

● Cut peppers open and discard stems and seeds. Cut the peppers into small pieces with scissors or a knife. Place in a bowl and pour boiling water over the pepper pieces. Let stand for 45 to 60 minutes or till pliable. Drain well.

1	2½- to 3-pound broiler-fryer chicken, cut up
	Salt
	Pepper
2	tablespoons cooking oil *or* shortening

● Meanwhile, rinse chicken, then pat dry. Season with salt and pepper. In a large skillet or Dutch oven cook chicken pieces in hot oil or shortening, uncovered, over medium heat for 10 to 15 minutes or till light brown, turning to brown evenly. Remove chicken from skillet or Dutch oven and set aside. Drain skillet or Dutch oven.

¾	cup chicken broth
1	medium tomato, peeled and cut up
¼	cup slivered almonds
¼	cup chopped onion
1	to 2 canned jalapeño peppers
2	tablespoons raisins
1	tablespoon sesame seed
2	cloves garlic
1	teaspoon sugar
½	teaspoon salt
⅛	teaspoon aniseed
⅛	teaspoon ground cinnamon
⅛	teaspoon ground coriander
⅛	teaspoon ground nutmeg
½	square (½ ounce) unsweetened chocolate

● For mole sauce, in a blender container or food processor bowl combine chicken broth, tomato, almonds, onion, jalapeño peppers, raisins, sesame seed, garlic, sugar, salt, aniseed, cinnamon, coriander, nutmeg, and drained peppers. Cover and blend or process to a coarse puree. Transfer sauce mixture to skillet or Dutch oven and add chocolate. Cook and stir over low heat to combine ingredients and melt chocolate.

	Hot cooked rice
2	tablespoons toasted slivered almonds

● Add chicken to sauce mixture in skillet or Dutch oven. Cover and simmer for 25 to 30 minutes or till chicken is tender, turning once.
　　To serve, transfer chicken to a serving platter with rice. Skim fat from sauce. Pour sauce over chicken and rice. Sprinkle with almonds. Makes 6 servings.

Moles (MOH-lays) and chocolate go together hand in glove. But a true mole isn't really a chocolate sauce. Only one small piece of chocolate goes into a large pot full of this dark-brown chili pepper concoction.
　　The specific dried pepper or combination of peppers you use (*not* the chocolate) determines the flavor of the mole sauce. The ancho is the most widely used pepper in Mexican cooking and gives moles a mild to medium hotness. The mulato pepper gives a slightly sweeter mole, but is harder to find. Pasilla peppers produce a more piquant mole that's a bit hotter than the ancho version.

Pork and Peppers

2 **pounds lean boneless pork, cut into 1-inch cubes** 2 **tablespoons cooking oil** 1 **large onion, thinly sliced and separated into rings** 2 **cloves garlic, minced** 1 **teaspoon ground cumin**	● In a large saucepan brown *half* of the pork in hot oil. With a slotted spoon, remove pork. Set aside. Add the remaining pork, onion, garlic, and cumin. Cook till meat is brown. Return all the pork to the saucepan.

3 *or* 4 **large Anaheim peppers,** *or* **two 4-ounce cans diced green chili peppers, drained** 5 *or* 6 **fresh tomatillos, chopped,** *or* **one 13-ounce can tomatillos, drained, rinsed, and cut up** 1 **cup chicken broth** 1 **large tomato, chopped** 1 **teaspoon dried oregano, crushed** 2 **teaspoons lime juice**	● If using fresh peppers, loosen skins by broiling peppers 4 inches from heat till charred on all sides, turning once. Place the charred peppers in a paper bag. Close the bag tightly and let stand for 10 minutes. Remove peppers from bag. Peel skin away from flesh and cut off stems. Slit peppers open and scrape away seeds and ribs; coarsely chop. Stir tomatillos, broth, peppers, tomato, and oregano into saucepan. Bring to boiling. Reduce heat and simmer, covered, about 1½ hours or till meat is tender. Uncover and boil gently for 20 to 30 minutes more or till slightly thickened, stirring occasionally. Stir in lime juice.

When buying fresh tomatillos, avoid the shriveled or bruised ones. To store them, refrigerate, unwashed, between paper towels for up to 4 weeks. Look for canned tomatillos in Latin American sections of larger supermarkets.

Hot cooked rice 2 **tablespoons toasted slivered almonds**	● To serve, spoon pork mixture over rice and sprinkle with toasted almonds. Makes 6 servings.

Chicken with Pumpkin Seed Sauce

2 **whole large chicken breasts (about 2½ pounds total), skinned, boned, and halved lengthwise** 3 **tablespoons all-purpose flour** 1 **beaten egg** ½ **cup fine dry bread crumbs** 2 **tablespoons butter** *or* **margarine**	● Roll chicken breasts in flour to coat. Dip in egg, then coat with bread crumbs. Heat butter or margarine in a medium skillet. Add chicken breasts and cook over low heat, uncovered, for 25 to 30 minutes or till chicken is tender, turning to brown evenly. Drain on paper towels.

Pumpkin Seed Sauce: In a blender container or food processor bowl combine one 13-ounce can *tomatillos,* drained and rinsed; 3 tablespoons *pumpkin seed;* 2 tablespoons sliced *almonds;* 1 tablespoon snipped *cilantro or parsley;* and 1 *jalapeño pepper,* seeded and coarsely chopped. Cover and blend or process to a coarse puree. Transfer to a saucepan. Heat through. Makes about 1 cup.

Pumpkin Seed Sauce (see recipe, right) **Snipped cilantro** *or* **parsley (optional)**	● To serve, arrange chicken breasts on a serving platter. Spoon Pumpkin Seed Sauce over chicken. Garnish with cilantro or parsley, if desired. Makes 4 servings.

Snapper Veracruz

1 pound fresh *or* frozen red snapper fillets *or* other fish fillets 3 medium potatoes (1 pound)	● Thaw fish, if frozen. Scrub potatoes, then peel and quarter them. Cook potatoes, covered, in boiling salted water for 20 to 25 minutes or till tender. Drain and keep warm.
¼ cup all-purpose flour ⅛ teaspoon salt ⅛ teaspoon pepper 1 tablespoon cooking oil	● Meanwhile, in a small mixing bowl stir together flour, salt, and pepper. Coat fish fillets on both sides with flour mixture. In a 10-inch skillet cook fillets in hot oil over medium heat for 4 to 5 minutes on each side or till fish flakes easily when tested with a fork. Remove fish from skillet and keep warm.
1 large onion, sliced and separated into rings 2 cloves garlic, minced 1 tablespoon cooking oil	● For sauce, in the skillet cook onion and garlic in hot cooking oil till onion is tender but not brown.
1 16-ounce can tomatoes, cut up ¼ cup sliced pimiento-stuffed olives ¼ cup dry white wine 2 tablespoons capers, drained 2 teaspoons seeded and chopped canned jalapeño pepper ½ teaspoon sugar 1 bay leaf Several dashes ground cinnamon	● Stir in *undrained* tomatoes, olives, wine, capers, jalapeño pepper, sugar, bay leaf, and cinnamon. Bring sauce mixture to boiling. Boil gently, uncovered, for 5 to 7 minutes or till mixture is slightly thickened. Add cooked fish fillets to sauce. Heat through. Remove bay leaf.
Snipped cilantro *or* parsley (optional)	● Arrange fish and potatoes on a serving platter. Spoon sauce atop. Garnish with cilantro or parsley, if desired. Makes 4 servings.

There are as many versions of this colorful dish as there are red snappers swimming in the Gulf of Mexico! Even so, no matter what recipe you use, the traditional tomato-base sauce should always be full of garlic, onion, peppers, and a hint of cinnamon. And don't forget the potatoes—they help cut the hotness from the peppers.

If you purchase Pacific snapper (also called rockfish) rather than red snapper, fry the fillets a minute or so longer to compensate for the extra thickness of the fillets.

Baked Chiles Rellenos

3 large poblano peppers *or* green peppers	● Halve peppers lengthwise and carefully remove stems, seeds, and veins.
6 ounces Monterey Jack, cheddar, Havarti, *or* mozzarella cheese	● Fill each pepper half with cheese, cutting cheese into pieces to fit. Place filled pepper halves, cut side up, in a well-greased 10x6x2-inch baking dish.
4 beaten eggs ⅓ cup milk ½ cup all-purpose flour ½ teaspoon baking powder ¼ teaspoon salt 1 cup shredded Monterey Jack, cheddar, Havarti, *or* mozzarella cheese (4 ounces)	● In a medium mixing bowl combine eggs and milk. Add flour, baking powder, and salt. Beat with a rotary beater till smooth. Pour egg mixture over peppers. Bake, uncovered, in a 450° oven for 15 minutes. Sprinkle with shredded cheese.
Red Chili Sauce *or* Green Chili Sauce (see recipes, page 27) Dairy sour cream	● Serve peppers with warm Red Chili Sauce or Green Chili Sauce and top with sour cream. Makes 6 main-dish servings.

We're *always* on the lookout for ways to streamline recipes and shorten the time you spend in the kitchen. This casserole version of the classic Chiles Rellenos (CHEE-lehs reh-YEH-nohs) is a good example. Rather than wrestle with the traditional method of dipping the stuffed chilies in batter and frying, we placed the stuffed chilies in a baking dish and poured the batter over the top—less work *and* less mess, but just as delicious.

Huevos Rancheros

2 tablespoons cooking oil 4 6-inch corn tortillas, 8-inch Flour Tortillas (see recipe, page 37), *or* purchased flour tortillas 8 eggs 1 tablespoon water	● In a heavy 12-inch skillet heat cooking oil. Fry each tortilla in hot oil for 10 seconds or till limp. Drain on paper towels. Keep tortillas warm in a 300° oven while preparing eggs. In same skillet reheat cooking oil. Carefully break eggs into skillet. When whites are set and edges cooked, add water. Cover skillet and cook eggs to desired doneness.
Ranchero Salsa (see recipe, page 26) *or* Green Chili Sauce (see recipe, page 27) ½ cup shredded Monterey Jack cheese (2 ounces) Avocado slices Cilantro *or* parsley sprigs	● Place tortillas on 4 dinner plates. Top *each* with *2* fried eggs. Spoon some warm Ranchero Salsa or Green Chili Sauce over each. Sprinkle with cheese. Garnish with avocado slices and cilantro or parsley. Serve immediately. Makes 4 servings.

When you hear Huevos Rancheros (WEH-vohs rahn-CHEH-rohs), don't automatically think breakfast. Instead, serve it with refried beans and a tossed salad for a great lunch or supper.

Dinner for Six

Update the flavors of Old Mexico with the creative cooking style of today. Because many of the foods can be made ahead, this elegant menu will impress your guests without leaving you exhausted.

MENU
Avocado Soup
Fiesta Chicken Roll-Ups
Spinach Salad with
  Garbanzo Beans
Flour tortillas
Almond Dessert
Pot Coffee con Leche

MENU COUNTDOWN
6 Hours Ahead or Day Before:
Prepare Avocado Soup; chill. Prepare salad dressing; chill. Pound and roll boned chicken breasts for Fiesta Chicken Roll-Ups; cover and chill.

1½ Hours Ahead:
Assemble vegetables for salad; chill. Coat, brown, and bake chicken and begin sauce for Fiesta Chicken Roll-Ups. Assemble ingredients for Almond Dessert. Dissolve brown sugar for Pot Coffee con Leche.

5 Minutes Ahead:
Wrap tortillas in foil; heat in a 400° oven. Drizzle dressing over salad; toss. Finish sauce for Fiesta Chicken Roll-Ups; pour over chicken.

During or After Meal:
Bake Almond Dessert. Steep Pot Coffee con Leche.

Almond Dessert
(see recipe, page 36)

Spinach Salad with Garbanzo Beans
(see recipe, page 34)

Avocado Soup
(see recipe, page 34)

Pot Coffee con Leche
(see recipe, page 37)

Fiesta Chicken Roll-Ups
(see recipe, page 35)

Avocado Soup

Pictured on page 32.

1	14½-ounce can chicken broth
2	medium avocados, seeded, peeled, and cut up
1	thin slice of a small onion
3	tablespoons lime juice
½	teaspoon salt

● In a blender container combine chicken broth, avocados, onion slice, lime juice, and salt; cover the blender container and blend till the mixture is smooth. Pour into a bowl.

| 1½ | cups milk |
| 1 | lime, cut into wedges (optional) |

● Stir in milk. Cover and chill thoroughly. If desired, serve with lime wedges. Makes 6 servings.

Soup usually is the first course of a large Mexican meal. Start your special dinner with this easy, creamy soup that you whirl in the blender. Make the soup ahead of time and chill it in the refrigerator until you're ready to serve it.

Spinach Salad With Garbanzo Beans

Pictured on pages 32–33.

3	tablespoons olive oil
2	tablespoons white wine vinegar
1	tablespoon water
1	clove garlic, minced
½	teaspoon salt
½	teaspoon brown sugar
¼	teaspoon dry mustard
¼	teaspoon dried thyme, crushed

● For dressing, in a screw-top jar combine oil, white wine vinegar, water, garlic, salt, brown sugar, dry mustard, and thyme. Cover and shake well. (To store dressing, chill in the refrigerator. Let stand at room temperature about 30 minutes before serving.)

6	cups torn fresh spinach (8 ounces)
1	15-ounce can garbanzo beans, drained
½	cup sliced radishes

● In a large bowl combine spinach, garbanzo beans, and radishes. Shake dressing and pour over salad; toss lightly to coat. Makes 6 servings.

Tossed salads, as Americans know them, are not common to most Mexican meals. Instead, garnishes of chopped lettuce, radishes, and onion usually replace the need for added greens. Salad-loving gringos, however, will find this salad a refreshing and fitting complement to the rest of the meal.

Fiesta Chicken Roll-Ups

Pictured on page 33.

3 whole large chicken breasts, skinned, halved lengthwise, and boned	● For each chicken roll, place a chicken breast half between 2 pieces of clear plastic wrap. Working from center to edge, use smooth side of a meat mallet to pound lightly to ⅛-inch thickness.
1 4-ounce can whole green chili peppers, rinsed and drained	● Remove wrap. Halve *three* peppers lengthwise; remove seeds. (Keep any remaining peppers for another use.) Place 1 pepper half on each chicken piece, as shown. Fold in sides of chicken; roll up jelly-roll style. Secure with wooden toothpicks. If desired, cover and chill for several hours or overnight.
¼ cup all-purpose flour **¼ cup yellow cornmeal** **Dash garlic powder** **Dash ground red pepper** **1 egg** **3 tablespoons milk**	● Combine ¼ cup flour, cornmeal, garlic powder, ground red pepper, and ¼ teaspoon *salt;* set aside. Beat together egg and 3 tablespoons milk. Roll each chicken roll in flour mixture; dip in egg mixture, then roll again in flour mixture.
¼ cup cooking oil	● In a skillet heat ¼ cup oil over medium heat. Cook chicken rolls in hot oil for 10 to 15 minutes, turning to brown all sides. Transfer chicken to a 12x7½x2-inch baking dish. Bake in a 400° oven for 15 to 17 minutes or till tender.
3 tablespoons cooking oil **2 tablespoons finely chopped onion** **2 cloves garlic, minced**	● Meanwhile, prepare sauce. In a 2-quart saucepan heat 3 tablespoons oil. Add onion and garlic; cook about 5 minutes or till tender but not brown.
1 7½-ounce can tomatoes, cut up **½ cup chicken broth** **2 tablespoons chili powder** **2 teaspoons vinegar** **¾ teaspoon crushed red pepper** **¼ teaspoon ground cumin** **¼ teaspoon dried oregano, crushed**	● Stir in the *undrained* tomatoes, chicken broth, chili powder, vinegar, crushed red pepper, ground cumin, dried oregano, and ¼ teaspoon *salt.* Simmer the mixture, uncovered, for 20 minutes. Transfer the baked chicken rolls to a serving platter. Remove toothpicks; keep chicken warm.
½ cup milk **2 tablespoons all-purpose flour**	● Combine ½ cup milk and 2 tablespoons flour; stir into tomato mixture. Cook and stir till thickened and bubbly. Cook and stir for 1 minute more.
½ cup shredded Monterey Jack *or* cheddar cheese **¼ cup sliced pitted ripe olives**	● To serve, pour sauce over chicken rolls; top with cheese and olives. Makes 6 servings.

The green chili peppers hidden inside these chicken rolls are mild, so you can serve this impressive entrée to both torrid and tender palates. If everyone at the table has a high tolerance for hot food, consider using green chili peppers that have "hot" on the label.

Place half of a seeded chili pepper on each pounded piece of chicken. If the chili peppers are too long, you may have to fold them under to keep them inside when you roll up the chicken.

Almond Dessert

Pictured on page 32.

1 cup slivered almonds	● Spread almonds in a single layer in a baking pan. Toast in a 350° oven about 10 minutes or till light brown, stirring often. Reserve *1 tablespoon*. Place remainder in a blender container. Cover and grind till fine; set aside.
¼ cup butter *or* margarine **1¾ cups sugar** **¾ cup water** **3 inches stick cinnamon**	● In a 1½-quart saucepan melt butter or margarine. Add sugar, water, and stick cinnamon; boil gently, uncovered, for 5 minutes. Remove from heat. Remove and discard stick cinnamon.
¼ cup dark rum	● Pour *half* of the sugar and butter mixture (about 1 cup) into a small bowl. Stir in the rum; set aside.
2 eggs	● Beat eggs slightly with a fork; mix into remaining half of the sugar and butter mixture. Stir in the ground toasted almonds. Return to heat. Cook and stir over low heat for 4 to 5 minutes or till thickened. Remove from heat.
1 10¾-ounce frozen loaf pound cake, thawed	● Cut pound cake crosswise into 18 slices about ½ inch thick. Dip 6 of the cake slices in the rum mixture and place on the bottom of an 8x8x2-inch baking dish. Spoon *one-third* of the almond mixture over cake slices. Repeat dipping and layering till there are 3 layers of cake and 3 layers of almond mixture. Bake, uncovered, in a 350° oven for 15 to 20 minutes or till light brown. Cool slightly.
½ cup dairy sour cream **¼ cup milk**	● Combine sour cream and milk. Cut baked dessert into serving pieces and place on individual plates. Top with sour cream mixture and reserved toasted almonds. Makes 6 servings.

Now for the perfect end to a perfect meal. Soak pound cake slices in rum-flavored syrup, layer with a ground almond mixture, and bake. For a crowning touch, top each rich serving with a satiny spoonful of sour cream topping and a sprinkling of toasted almonds.

Pot Coffee

Pictured on page 33.

6 cups water ¼ cup packed brown sugar 3 inches stick cinnamon 6 whole cloves	● In a 3-quart saucepan combine water, brown sugar, stick cinnamon, and cloves; heat and stir till sugar is dissolved.
¾ cup regular-grind, roasted coffee	● Add coffee. Bring to boiling; reduce heat. Simmer, uncovered, for 1 to 2 minutes. Remove from heat. Cover and let stand for 15 minutes. Strain before serving. Makes 6 (8-ounce) servings.
	Pot Coffee con Leche: Pour equal amounts of *Pot Coffee* and *warm milk* into each cup. Add sugar to taste.

Ignore your percolator or coffee maker when brewing this traditional Mexican coffee. Steep the coffee and spices with water in a saucepan and strain before serving. If the strainer you use does not have a fine mesh, line the inside of the strainer with several layers of cheesecloth to keep the coffee grounds from seeping through the holes.

Make Your Own Flour Tortillas

Like homemade bread, homemade flour tortillas taste fresher than tortillas from the supermarket. What's more, they're as easy to make as biscuits.

Stir together 2 cups *all-purpose flour,* 1 teaspoon *salt,* and 1 teaspoon *baking powder.* Cut in 2 tablespoons *shortening* till mixture resembles cornmeal. Gradually add ½ to ¾ cup *warm water;* mix till the dough forms a ball. Knead 15 to 20 times. Let stand for 15 minutes.

For 8-inch tortillas, divide dough into 12 equal portions. (For 10-inch tortillas, divide dough into 8 portions.) Shape into balls. On a lightly floured surface or between 2 pieces of waxed paper, roll each ball into an 8-inch (or 10-inch) circle. Cook on a medium-hot ungreased griddle or skillet about 25 seconds or till puffy. Turn and cook about 25 seconds more or till the edges curl slightly. Makes 12 (8-inch) tortillas or 8 (10-inch) tortillas.

Fried Ice Cream

1 pint ice cream	● Place 4 scoops (about ½ cup each) of ice cream in a small pan. Freeze for 1 hour or till firm.
1 beaten egg **¼ teaspoon vanilla** **2½ cups sweetened corn flakes, crushed** **½ teaspoon ground cinnamon**	● In a small mixing bowl stir together egg and vanilla. In a pie plate carefully stir together cereal and cinnamon. 　Dip each frozen ice-cream ball in the egg mixture, then roll it in cereal mixture. Return coated ice-cream balls to pan and freeze for 1 hour or till firm. Reserve remaining cereal mixture.
1 beaten egg **¼ teaspoon vanilla**	● In a small mixing bowl stir together egg and vanilla. Remove coated ice-cream balls from the freezer. Dip balls in egg mixture, then roll them in remaining cereal mixture. Return to pan. Cover and freeze for several hours or till firm.
Cooking oil for deep-fat frying **Whipped cream (optional)** **Mint sprigs (optional)**	● In a deep-fat fryer or heavy saucepan fry frozen, coated ice-cream balls, 1 or 2 at a time, in deep hot oil (375°) for 15 seconds or till golden brown. Drain on paper towels. Return the fried ice-cream balls to the freezer while frying the remaining balls. Serve immediately with whipped cream and garnish with mint, if desired. Makes 4 servings.

Dip the frozen ice-cream balls in the egg mixture, then roll them in the cereal mixture. Make sure the cereal completely covers the ice cream.

Place the four coated ice-cream balls in a small pan (or on a baking sheet) and put them into the freezer till they're firm.

Fry the ice-cream balls in hot oil about 15 seconds or till golden. Drain well on paper towels. Serve the fried ice-cream balls immediately with whipped cream and a mint sprig, or try them with jam or ice-cream topping.

Buñuelos

2 cups all-purpose flour 1 teaspoon baking powder ½ teaspoon salt ¼ teaspoon cream of tartar 2 tablespoons shortening 2 beaten eggs ⅓ cup milk	● In a mixing bowl stir together flour, baking powder, salt, and cream of tartar. Cut in shortening till thoroughly combined. Make a well in center. In a small mixing bowl combine eggs and milk. Add to flour mixture all at once. Stir just till dough clings together.	**Don't wait till December to eat buñuelos (boon-WAY-lohs), a favorite Mexican Christmas treat. Serve these fried sugar tortillas year-round with ice cream.**
	● On a lightly floured surface knead dough about 2 minutes or till smooth. Divide dough into 24 equal portions, then shape into balls. Cover dough and let rest for 15 to 20 minutes.	
Cooking oil Cinnamon-Sugar Syrup *or* Cinnamon Sugar	● In a heavy 10-inch skillet heat about ¾ inch of cooking oil to 375°. Meanwhile, on a lightly floured surface roll each ball into a 4-inch circle. Fry circles, one at a time, in hot oil for 1 to 1½ minutes on each side or till golden. Drain on paper towels. Drizzle with Cinnamon-Sugar Syrup or sprinkle with Cinnamon Sugar. Make and serve the same day. Makes 24.	
	● **Cinnamon-Sugar Syrup:** In a small saucepan combine ½ cup *sugar*, ¼ cup packed *brown sugar*, ¼ cup *water*, 1 tablespoon *corn syrup*, and 3 inches *stick cinnamon* or dash ground *cinnamon*. Bring to boiling. Reduce heat and boil gently, without stirring, about 20 minutes or till thick. Discard cinnamon stick. Makes about ⅔ cup syrup.	**Be sure to serve the syrup warm, as it hardens when cooled and is difficult to reheat. Start to make the syrup while the balls of dough rest.**
	● **Cinnamon Sugar:** In a small mixing bowl stir together ½ cup *sugar* and 1 teaspoon ground *cinnamon*.	

Sopaipillas

2 cups all-purpose flour 1 tablespoon baking powder ½ teaspoon salt 1 tablespoon shortening ⅔ cup warm water (110° to 115°)	● In a medium mixing bowl stir together flour, baking powder, and salt. Cut in shortening till thoroughly combined. Gradually add water, stirring with a fork (dough will be crumbly).	Take it from our Test Kitchen: The secret to making these "pillows" of bread is having the oil *very* hot and frying just a couple at a time.
	● On a lightly floured surface knead dough for 3 to 5 minutes or till smooth. Divide dough in half. Cover and let dough rest for 10 minutes. Roll each dough half into a 12½x10-inch rectangle. Using a fluted pastry wheel or knife, cut twenty 2½-inch squares from each half (do not reroll or patch dough).	
Cooking oil for deep-fat frying Sifted powdered sugar Honey (optional)	● In a heavy 3-quart saucepan fry squares, 1 or 2 at a time, in deep hot oil (425°) for 30 to 40 seconds on each side or till golden. Drain on paper towels. Sprinkle with powdered sugar. Serve warm or cool with honey, if desired. Makes 40.	

Mexican Doughnut Strips

1 cup water
¼ cup butter *or* margarine
1 tablespoon sugar
¼ teaspoon salt
1 cup all-purpose flour
2 eggs
	● Bring water, butter or margarine, sugar, and salt to boiling. Add flour all at once, stirring vigorously. Cook and stir with a wooden spoon till mixture forms a ball that doesn't separate. Remove from heat and cool for 10 minutes.
	    Add the eggs, one at a time, beating well after each addition with the wooden spoon till smooth.
		Street vendors sell these light and crispy pastries at festivals and markets throughout Mexico.
		    At *your* house, try them with a mug of steaming hot chocolate.

	● Spoon dough into a pastry bag fitted with a large star tip. Pipe the dough into strips 3 inches long and ¾ inch wide onto a baking sheet lined with waxed paper. Freeze strips about 20 minutes or till they can be pulled off waxed paper. (Do not remove any strips from freezer till you're ready to fry them.)	
Cooking oil for deep-fat frying Sugar	● In a heavy 3-quart saucepan fry dough strips, a few at a time, in deep hot oil (375°) for 3 to 4 minutes or till golden brown, turning occasionally. Drain on paper towels. Roll in sugar while warm. Makes 24.	

Marinated Seafood

Pictured at right and on the cover.

8 ounces large fresh *or* frozen peeled and deveined shrimp 8 ounces fresh *or* frozen scallops	● Thaw shrimp and scallops, if frozen. Cut any large scallops in half. 　In a medium saucepan cook shrimp and scallops in boiling water about 1 minute or till shrimp turns pink and scallops are opaque. Drain and rinse under cool water to stop cooking.
½ cup lime *or* lemon juice ¼ cup water	● Put shrimp and scallops into a plastic bag, then set bag in a bowl. 　For marinade, stir together lime or lemon juice and water. Pour marinade over seafood in bag. Close bag tightly, then turn to evenly distribute the marinade. Chill for 8 hours or overnight, turning bag occasionally.
¼ cup sliced green onion 1 4-ounce can diced green chili peppers, drained 3 tablespoons olive oil *or* cooking oil 1 to 2 tablespoons snipped cilantro *or* parsley 1 tablespoon capers, drained	● Drain shrimp and scallops, discarding marinade. In a medium mixing bowl stir together green onion, chili peppers, oil, cilantro or parsley, capers, dash *salt*, and dash *pepper*. Gently stir in shrimp and scallops till combined. Cover and chill for at least 2 hours.
1 medium tomato, seeded and chopped (optional) 4 thin slices red onion, halved	● Just before serving, toss tomato with seafood mixture, if desired. Arrange halved onion slices around edge of a serving platter. (Place rounded edge of onion out.) Spoon seafood mixture into center. Makes 6 servings.

Make individual servings of this first-course appetizer by arranging *four* halved onion slices around the edges of each of *six* individual plates. Spoon some of the seafood mixture into the center, then garnish with thin avocado slices and lime wedges, if you like.

Cheese Quesadillas

Cheese Quesadillas are pictured opposite and on the cover.

2 cups shredded Monterey Jack, cheddar, Swiss, *or* mozzarella cheese 6 8-inch Flour Tortillas (see recipe, page 37) *or* purchased flour tortillas 1 4-ounce can diced green chili peppers, drained	● Sprinkle ⅓ cup cheese on half of *each* tortilla. Top with chili peppers. Fold tortillas in half, pressing down gently. 　In a large skillet or griddle cook tortillas, 2 at a time, over medium-high heat about 4 minutes total or till cheese melts, turning once. Remove tortillas from skillet or griddle and keep warm.
Guacamole (see recipe, page 22) Sliced pitted ripe olives Homemade Salsa (see recipe, page 24) (optional)	● Cut tortillas into 3 triangles. Serve with Guacamole, olives, and Homemade Salsa, if desired. Makes 6 servings.

Chorizo and Cheese Quesadillas: Prepare as directed at left *except*, using a total of ½ pound *Homemade Chorizo* (see recipe, page 10) *or bulk chorizo,* cooked and drained, sprinkle a little over half of *each* tortilla. Sprinkle 1 cup shredded *cheddar cheese* over chorizo. Fold tortillas in half. Cook and serve as directed at left.

Cheese Quesadillas

Cheese Crisps
(see recipe, page 44)

Marinated Seafood

Jalapeño Nachos

4 cups tortilla chips ½ of a 16-ounce can refried beans ¼ cup Picante Sauce (see recipe, page 26) *or* purchased salsa	● Arrange chips about 1 layer deep (overlapping slightly) on an 11- or 12-inch ovenproof platter. In a small saucepan combine refried beans and Picante Sauce or salsa. Cook and stir just till heated through. Immediately spoon bean mixture over chips.	**Meaty Nachos: Cook ½ pound *ground beef*, *Homemade Chorizo* (see recipe, page 10), *or bulk chorizo* till brown. Drain well. Stir in ⅓ cup *Picante Sauce or* purchased *salsa* and heat through. Arrange tortilla chips on an ovenproof platter as directed at left. Drizzle meat mixture over chips. Top with 1½ cups shredded *cheddar or American cheese*. Bake as directed at left.**
1 medium tomato, chopped 2 tablespoons to ¼ cup chopped jalapeño peppers ¾ cup shredded Monterey Jack cheese (3 ounces) ¾ cup shredded cheddar cheese (3 ounces)	● Sprinkle tomato and jalapeño peppers evenly over chips. Top with cheeses. Bake in a 425° oven for 2 to 3 minutes or till cheese melts. Serve immediately. Makes 8 servings.	

Cheese Crisps

Pictured on page 43 and on the cover.

1 cup all-purpose flour ½ teaspoon baking powder ¼ teaspoon salt 1½ teaspoons shortening *or* lard ¼ to ⅓ cup warm water (110° to 115°)	● For tortillas, in a medium mixing bowl stir together flour, baking powder, and salt. Cut in shortening or lard till thoroughly combined. Gradually add warm water and toss together till dough can be gathered into a ball (if necessary, add more water, 1 teaspoon at a time). Knead dough 15 to 20 times. Let dough rest for 15 minutes. Divide dough in half and shape into balls.	**When time runs short, make these appetizer Mexican-style pizzas with a couple of packaged 10-inch flour tortillas.** **Crisp them in a 350° oven about 8 minutes, sprinkle with toppings, and bake for 5 minutes more.**
	● On a lightly floured surface, use a rolling pin to flatten each ball of dough into a 10-inch circle. Place the 2 tortillas on lightly greased baking sheets or pizza pans. Bake in a 350° oven for 15 to 20 minutes or till crisp and lightly browned.	
1 cup shredded Monterey Jack cheese (4 ounces) 1 cup shredded cheddar cheese (4 ounces) 1 medium tomato, chopped 3 tablespoons sliced green onion 2 tablespoons diced canned green chili peppers, drained	● Sprinkle cheeses evenly over the 2 tortillas. Top each with tomato, onion, and chili peppers. Bake about 5 minutes more or till cheese is bubbly. Remove from oven and cut into wedges. Makes 2.	

Frozen Margaritas

¾ cup tequila 1 6-ounce can frozen limeade concentrate ½ cup orange liqueur	● In a blender container combine the tequila, limeade concentrate, and orange liqueur. Cover and blend till smooth.

30 to 35 ice cubes
    (about 4 cups)
    Lime slices
	● With blender running, add the ice cubes, one at a time, through hole in lid, blending till slushy. Serve in salt-rimmed glasses* garnished with lime slices. Makes about 8 (4-ounce) servings.
	***Note:** To prepare glasses, rub the rim of each glass with a little *lime juice* or a *lime wedge.* Invert glasses into a shallow dish of coarse *salt.* Shake off excess salt.

Though its Mexican origins are questioned by some, most of us take for granted that the margarita is the national drink of Mexico. We probably owe the creation of the libation to the custom of drinking straight tequila with salt and a wedge of lime, but a more delightful legend tells of the cocktail being invented by a man for his wife, Margarita.

Sangrita

6 medium tomatoes (about
    2 pounds), peeled,
    seeded, and coarsely cut
    up, *or* one 28-ounce can
    tomatoes
⅓ cup lime juice
1 slice of a medium onion
1 jalapeño pepper,
    seeded and cut up
1 teaspoon sugar
    Several dashes bottled hot
    pepper sauce
	● In a blender container place fresh tomatoes or *undrained* canned tomatoes, lime juice, onion, jalapeño pepper, sugar, and hot pepper sauce. Cover and blend till smooth.

1 cup orange juice
⅓ cup tequila
    Ice cubes
    Celery stalks
	● Strain mixture through a sieve lined with cheesecloth. Transfer to a serving pitcher. Stir in orange juice and tequila. Serve over ice cubes with celery stalks. Makes 7 to 9 (4-ounce) servings.

Follow this Mexican version of a Bloody Mary with a tequila chaser, then suck on a lime wedge for a refresher—now *that's* the way they do it south of the border!

Sangria

½ cup sugar
½ cup water
1 lemon, cut into ¼-inch-thick slices
1 orange, cut into ¼-inch-thick slices

● For syrup, in a small saucepan combine sugar, water, and the 4 end slices from the lemon and the orange. Bring to boiling, stirring till sugar dissolves. Remove from heat and cool.
  Squeeze juice from cooked fruit slices into the syrup, then discard.

1 750-milliliter bottle dry red wine, chilled
½ of a 32-ounce bottle carbonated water, chilled (2 cups)
2 tablespoons brandy
  Ice cubes

● In a large pitcher or bowl combine syrup, wine, carbonated water, brandy, and remaining fruit slices. Pour over ice in wine glasses. Makes about 12 (4-ounce) servings.

This fruity Spanish punch, bolstered with brandy, is just the thing to take the edge off Jalapeño Nachos (see recipe, page 44) or any other spicy tidbit.

Mexican Eggnog

2 cups light cream
1 cup milk
½ cup sugar

● In a large saucepan combine cream, milk, and sugar. Heat almost to boiling, stirring occasionally. *Do not boil.*

6 egg yolks

● Meanwhile, in a large mixer bowl beat egg yolks about 6 minutes or till thick and lemon colored. Gradually stir about *1 cup* of the hot cream mixture into egg yolks, then return all to saucepan. Cook and stir over low heat for 10 to 12 minutes or till mixture starts to thicken and coats a metal spoon. Cool mixture immediately by placing saucepan in a sink filled with ice water. Stir till cooled.

½ cup rum *or* brandy
½ teaspoon vanilla
  Ground cinnamon
  Ground toasted almonds *or* cashews (optional)

● Stir in rum or brandy and vanilla, then chill for at least 24 hours.
  Serve in small glasses, sprinkled with cinnamon and ground nuts, if desired. Makes about 8 (4-ounce) servings.

Mexican cooks offer this drink as an after-dinner liqueur and serve it in tiny cordial glasses.

Tequila Sunrise

1⅓ cups orange juice
½ cup tequila
¼ cup lime juice
  Ice cubes
2 tablespoons grenadine syrup
  Carambola, sliced and seeds removed (optional)

● In a small pitcher combine orange juice, tequila, and lime juice. Pour over ice in glasses. Slowly add *1½ teaspoons* grenadine syrup to *each* glass and let it sink to the bottom.
  Garnish with carambola, if desired. Stir before drinking. Makes about 4 (4-ounce) servings.

Pour the grenadine syrup *slowly* into each glass so it sinks to the bottom, leaving the orange juice mixture floating on top. Now *that's* a sunrise!

Tequila Cooler

3 cups unsweetened pineapple juice
2 cups unsweetened grapefruit juice
1 cup tequila
3 tablespoons grenadine syrup
  Ice cubes

● In a large pitcher combine pineapple juice, grapefruit juice, tequila, and grenadine. Pour over ice in chilled glasses. Garnish with mint sprigs, if desired. Makes about 6 (8-ounce) servings.

Just a few sips of this Tequila Cooler and your mind will take you on a carefree vacation in sunny Acapulco—ahhhh!

Tequila!

Mexico and tequila—you can't have one without the other! Tequila's claim to fame is the margarita, and that cocktail's popularity is making a name for tequila outside Mexico.

There are several types of tequila. Clear tequila, known as *white* or *silver,* comes out a powerful 104 to 106 proof after fermentation. Water is added to reduce it to 80 or 86 proof. Other varieties are aged in oak vats. The resulting pale-yellow color gives them the name *gold*. White and gold tequilas are used for cocktails. (Just for the record, this liquor is distilled from the *agave* plant, *not* the cactus.)

The very best tequila is amber-colored *añejo*. It should be served straight or on the rocks.

Similar to tequila, but made in a different region of Mexico, is *mezcal.* Although this fiery concoction isn't too common outside Mexico, some brands can be purchased in the U.S. If you've ever seen a liquor bottle with a worm in the bottom, you've seen a bottle of mezcal! This agave-root worm is said to give strength to anyone brave enough to gulp it down.

Index